PREPARE FOR MARS

MISSION: MARS

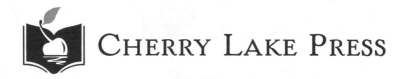

Published in the United States of America by Cherry Lake Publishing
Ann Arbor, Michigan
www.cherrylakepublishing.com

Reading Adviser: Beth Walker Gambro, MS, Ed., Reading Consultant, Yorkville, IL
Book Designer: Book Buddy Media
Photo Credits: page 1: ©Flashinmirror / Shutterstock; page 5: ©MARK GARLICK/SCIENCE
PHOTO LIBRARY / Getty Images; page 7: ©Stocktrek Images / Getty Images; page 9:
©MARK GARLICK/SCIENCE PHOTO LIBRARY / Getty Images; page 10: ©NASA/
JPL-Caltech / nasa.gov; page 13: ©NASA/JPL-Caltech / nasa.gov; page 15: ©NASA/JPL-
Caltech / nasa.gov; page 17: ©NASA/JPL-Caltech / nasa.gov; page 19: ©mkarco / Shutterstock;
page 21: ©NASA / nasa.gov; page 23: ©NASA/JPL / nasa.gov; page 25: ©John Brown / Getty
Images; page 27: ©Tobias Titz / Getty Images; page 28: ©Stocktrek Images / Getty Images;
page 29: ©Puntasit Choksawatdikorn / EyeEm / Getty Images; page 30: ©USGS Astrogeology
Science Center, Goddard Space Flight Center, NASA / usgs.gov

Cherry Lake Press is an imprint of Cherry Lake Publishing Group.

Library of Congress Cataloging-in-Publication Data has been filed and is available
at catalog.loc.gov

Cherry Lake Publishing would like to acknowledge the work of the Partnership for
21st Century Learning, a Network of Battelle for Kids.
Please visit *http://www.battelleforkids.org/networks/p21* for more information.

Printed in the United States of America
Corporate Graphics

ABOUT THE AUTHOR

Mari Bolte is a children's book author and editor. Streaming sci-if on TV is more her
speed, but tracking our planet's progress across the sky is still exciting! She lives in
Minnesota with her husband, daughter, and a house full of (non-Martian!) pets.

TABLE OF CONTENTS

Destination: Mars

On any given day, Mars is around 140 million miles away (225 million kilometers) from Earth. The goal of someday **colonizing** Mars is one that scientists and science-fiction fans have thought about for decades. The two planets have a lot in common.

But Mars is not a second Earth. There are many extreme conditions that pose a challenge to anyone planning to visit. Freezing cold temperatures and little oxygen are just the start. Dust storms, volcanoes, **craters**, and dunes cover the planet's surface. What else is out there?

Scientists have been observing dust storms on Mars for more than 100 years.

The first thing people think about when they hear "Mars" is the color. Its orange-red color is caused by its iron-heavy, dusty surface. Dust storms are common occurrences on the Red Planet. The fine, slightly metallic dust covers everything, burying anything in its way. The storms on Mars are different from storms on Earth. Mars has a thinner atmosphere. This means that a hurricane on Mars will feel like a light breeze on Earth. But the storms on Mars are huge. Every decade, there is a huge storm that covers the whole planet.

HiRISE

NASA launched the High Resolution Imaging Experiment (HiRISE) in 2005 on board the Reconnaissance Orbiter spacecraft. The orbiter is 125 to 250 miles (201 to 402 km) above the planet's surface. It is the most powerful camera sent into space. Since HiRISE arrived in 2006, it has sent nearly 70,000 images of Mars back to Earth. It helped scientists select landing sites for future rovers to explore. It has taken photos of the same place at different times, showing scientists how an area changes over time. It also keeps an eye on the Mars rovers. In 2021, it kept track of the Perseverance rover's progress on the planet.

Mars looks like a red marble. But it is not a perfect sphere! The Tharsis Rise is a 3,000-mile-wide (4,828 km) bump that sticks out 4 miles (6.4 km) from the planet's surface. Olympus Mons, Mars's tallest volcano, is part of Tharsis. It stands more than 15.5 miles (26 km) above the planet's surface. Earth has a similar area in Ecuador. The Andes Mountains are right on Earth's equator. Mount Chimborazo stands 3.9 miles (6.3 km) high. But Mars is only about half the size of Earth, which makes the Tharsis Rise even more impressive.

The surface of Mars isn't flat. It isn't smooth, either. Circular depressions called impact craters cover the planet's surface. They are caused by meteorites or other objects hitting the

Olympus Mons is about the size of the state of Arizona and is almost three times taller than Mount Everest.

planet at high speeds. More than 635,000 impact craters at least 0.6 miles (1 km) wide cover the planet's surface. Fewer than 200 craters like this have been found on Earth. That doesn't mean more didn't exist at one time. On Earth, water, sand, or lava from volcanoes might fill the craters to make a lake. Wind or **erosion** might wear down the sides. Scientists aren't sure how many craters on Earth have yet to be discovered.

Some of Mars's **terrain** is made up of interconnected ridges and dips that resemble the wrinkles and crannies in a brain. The brain terrain is found around the mid-latitude region of the planet. This is the area above and below the planet's equator. Some experts believe that the ridges are caused by frozen water changing directly into a gas just below the planet's surface.

Traveling Through Space

Although humans have not yet set foot on Mars, scientists have been taking the steps needed to get there eventually. Each mission to Mars has made human colonization a little more possible.

In 1962, the first *Mariner* spacecraft was built. There would eventually be 10 spacecraft total in this program. They were designed to visit Venus, Mars, and Mercury. *Mariner 4* was the first to make a successful **flyby** to Mars, taking the first photos on July 14, 1965. The photos were stored on a sound-recording device called a tape recorder. It took 4 days to transmit the photos back to Earth. *Mariner 6, Mariner 7*, and *Mariner 9* also had successful launches to Mars.

[21ST CENTURY SKILLS LIBRARY]

Timeline to Mars

1960: Russia attempts to launch the first Mars flyby, with *Marsnik 1* and *Marsnik 2.*

1965: NASA's *Mariner 4* is the first successful flyby.

1969: *Mariner 6* and *Mariner 7* achieve successful flybys.

1971: *Mariner 9* successfully **orbits** Mars.

1976: *Viking 1* and *Viking 2* orbit and land on Mars.

1997: *Mars Global Surveyor* orbits Mars.

1997: *Pathfinder* arrives with *Sojourner,* the first Mars rover, on board.

2004: The rovers *Spirit* and *Opportunity* land on Mars.

2005: The *Mars Reconnaissance Orbiter* is launched; it carries the HiRISE camera.

2007: *Phoenix* is launched; the probe's mission is to study the history of water on Mars.

2011: The *Mars Science Laboratory* is launched; it carries the rover *Curiosity.*

2013: *Mars Atmosphere and Volatile EvolutioN (MAVEN)* spacecraft orbiter is launched; its mission is to study the upper atmosphere of Mars.

2018: *InSight* touches down to study the planet's interior.

2021: The rover *Perseverance* lands on Mars; the drone *Ingenuity* makes the first powered flight.

Not every mission has been a success, but each successful mission has taught us more about Mars.

InSight took daily measurements of the planet's temperature, air and wind pressure, wind direction, and sunlight levels.

In 1975, NASA launched *Viking 1* and *Viking 2*. It was the first U.S. mission to land spacecraft on Mars and send images back. Each *Viking* spacecraft was both a lander and an orbiter. The lander and orbiter flew together. Once they reached Mars, they separated, with the landers making their way to the planet's surface. The landers looked for possible signs of life. Both found chemical evidence that suggested that life could have existed.

[21ST CENTURY SKILLS LIBRARY]

Surviving on Mars

All living things need water to survive. Explorers would have to bring water along on the way to Mars. But water is heavy and takes up a lot of room. On the International Space Station (ISS), about 80 percent of the water is recycled. Recycled water comes from urine, sweat, and condensation. After being filtered, the water is safe to drink.

A sustainable source of water would need to be found. Researchers believe Mars has a lot of ice that could be mined. But liquid water would not last long. The lower air pressure means water would quickly turn into gas. Engineers would need to find a way to harvest it.

InSight landed in 2018. It is equipped with instruments designed to explore underground. A seismometer takes the planet's "pulse," recording vibrations made by marsquakes and meteorite impacts. It may also be able to find signs of liquid water or active volcanoes. A heat **probe** burrows 16 feet (5 meters) into the planet's surface. It measures how much heat flows through the planet, and where it is coming from.

Skills on Mars

Perseverance's sample collection is part of the proposed Mars Sample Return mission. At a later date, a rover will be sent to retrieve the samples. Then a Mars Ascent Vehicle will launch the samples into orbit. An Earth Return Orbiter will pick up the samples in space. Finally, they will make their way back to Earth by the early 2030s. This sounds like our mail system, with a few extra steps added! Explorers to Mars will want a way to send and receive mail. Scientists will just need to figure out how to speed up deliveries!

The *Mars Science Laboratory* launched in 2011. Landing on August 5, 2012, it proved that a precise landing, and a landing with a large, heavy rover, was possible. The rover it carried, *Curiosity*, found proof that liquid water had been present in the past. It also discovered that Mars had the right chemical makeup to support **microbes**.

[21ST CENTURY SKILLS LIBRARY]

Perseverance was built in a clean, sterilized room to keep it from carrying microbes from Earth along to Mars.

Rovers use tools called science instruments to make observations and take detailed photos of rocks on Mars. *Perseverance* is the first rover to take samples to be studied later. The rover carries all the equipment and supplies needed for gathering samples. It then seals the samples and leaves them in a well-marked place. A future mission will collect the samples and bring them back to Earth.

X Marks the Spot

The first landers did not have much information about the planet's surface. The *Viking* probes orbited the planet before landing. They took images of potential landing sites, and then picked the places that looked safest.

Now that they have more data, scientists put a lot of thought into landing sites. Mars is full of unusual and unknown terrain that could make exploration difficult, or even deadly, for a rover. Even "safe" locations, such as the Jezero Crater, which is where *Perseverance* landed, was full of rocks, dunes, and steep crater walls. About half the planet is unsuitable for landing. Almost all the successful landings have occurred on the plains around Mars's equator.

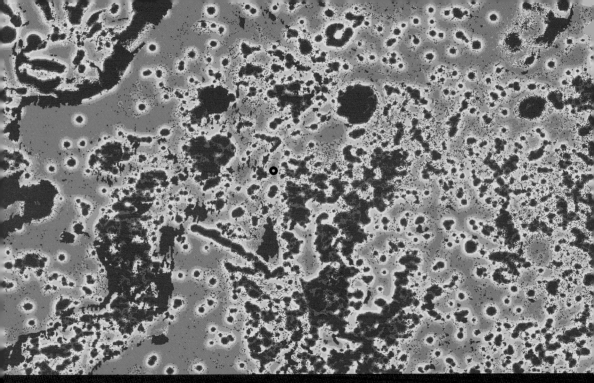

The red-colored hazards on the map include large boulders, jagged cliffs, and high dunes.

Safety Precautions

Perseverance *used a* **hazard map** *to help it land. The map showed hazardous places in red, and safer places in blue and green. As the rover landed, it used a Terrain-Relative Navigation System to compare the terrain to what was shown on the map. Then it decided if any adjustments needed to be made. The navigation system was accurate within 200 feet (61 m). Many hours of field testing were done to ensure the highest possible odds of success. But even so, there was still a risk that the rover would land somewhere unsuitable.*

Saturn

Saturn is the sixth planet in our solar system, and the second largest. It is nine times larger than Earth. If Earth was the size of a nickel, Saturn would be the size of a volleyball. Its rings, which are made of rock and ice, make it stand out. The planet is also a gas giant, made up of mainly hydrogen and helium, with a dense metallic **core***. Saturn is the planet farthest away that can be seen with the naked human eye. Ancient Romans named it for their god of agriculture and wealth.*

Phoenix was the only spacecraft to land in the Martian arctic. Its mission was to study the history of water there, the soil, and see if it might be habitable. It lasted 5 months in the arctic. In the winter, temperatures can reach –220 degrees Fahrenheit (–140 degrees Celsius). The Sun's rays do not reach the poles, either. *Phoenix* used **solar power** to run. Eventually, it ran out of power.

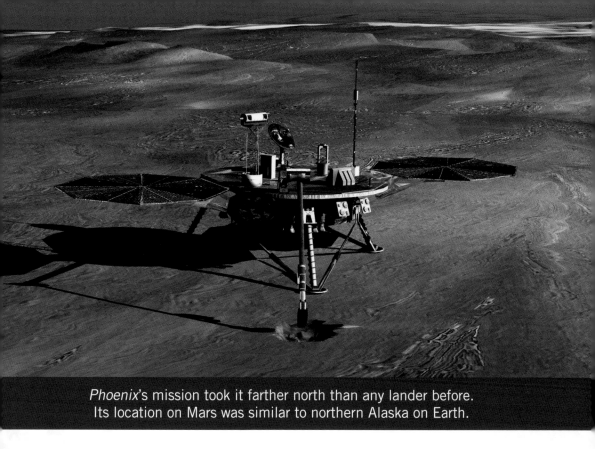

Phoenix's mission took it farther north than any lander before. Its location on Mars was similar to northern Alaska on Earth.

It sounds like an easy task to move to a new site if the original landing site is too steep or rocky. But even if they have a successful landing in a dangerous site, rovers do not move quickly. *Spirit* and *Opportunity* were the fastest rovers at 0.1 miles (0.16 km) per hour. It took *Opportunity* 11 years and 2 months to travel 26.2 miles (42.2 km), or the distance of a marathon. Human runners can finish a marathon in around 4.5 hours on foot!

Exploring the Planet

Exploring a new place means things won't be easy. There will be challenges that astronauts have never faced before. Traveling so far through space, living on a new planet, exploring unknown terrain, and looking for Martian life will all be new experiences. No matter how many times a thing is tested, there is always a risk that another thing will not go as planned. And because the gravity and atmosphere are so different on Mars, some things can't be fully tested. Sometimes scientists rely on simulations to test an idea.

[21ST CENTURY SKILLS LIBRARY]

140 MILLION MILES*

*225 MILLION KILOMETERS

The trip from Earth to Mars takes spacecraft between 150 and 300 days.

With 140 million miles (225 million km) between Earth and Mars, there is a lot that could go wrong on the way. Nearly 50 spacecraft have been launched to the Red Planet since 1960. Some did not even leave Earth's orbit. Others missed their target, were lost on the way, or landed and then immediately stopped working. And none of those spacecraft had people on board. Historically, missions to Mars only have about a 40 to 50 percent success rate.

Similar Science

The first Moon missions took place in 1958. Russia sent three Luna spacecraft into space. Luna 2 was the first to land on the Moon safely, in 1959. Over the next few years, NASA launched five Lunar orbiter missions to take photos of the Moon's surface. The orbiters helped scientists figure out potential landing sites. By 1972, NASA launched 11 Apollo missions and sent 24 astronauts to the Moon's surface or orbit. Today, the Artemis program is working to do the same thing, first on the Moon and then, hopefully, on Mars.

Another challenge to tackle in space is mental and physical health. It can take between 6 hours and up to 3 days for astronauts to get to the ISS. Usually ISS missions last around 6 months. It can take 7 to 9 months just to get to Mars! Think about how long a car or bus ride can seem. Then imagine you are in the car or bus with the same 3 to 6 people—for more than half a year! Mental health in space is important to think about.

More than 240 people from 19 countries have visited the International Space Station. It has been continuously occupied since November 2000.

On the ISS, astronauts exercise for around 2 hours a day. But because there is no gravity in space, they need specially designed equipment to make sure they actually get a workout! It would be fun to do a one-armed pull-up without any help! But it wouldn't do your body much good. Without exercise, your muscles get weak. Even astronauts on a strict program lose muscle tone. On just a 5- to 11-day mission, they lose up to 20 percent of their muscle mass.

By the Numbers

Communication is limited by the speed of light, which is around 186,000 miles (299,337 km) per second. On Earth, the limit isn't noticeable. But the farther from Earth you get, the longer the delay. The Moon is 238,855 miles (384,000 km) away. It takes around 1.3 seconds for light to travel that distance. On average, Mars is 140 million miles (225 million km) away, or 12.5 minutes at light speed. Pluto is 3 billion miles (4.6 billion km) away. A signal between Pluto and Earth would take 4.5 hours to receive!

No matter how much prep we do on Earth, something is bound to go wrong once we get to Mars. Think about the last time you went on vacation. Did you forget anything? Missions to the ISS can be resupplied by cargo vehicles. If something goes wrong, the astronauts can be back to Earth the same day. But once you're on your way to Mars, there's no turning around. There's probably only enough fuel for a one-way trip.

Scientists are always looking for new ways to enhance communication between Earth and Mars.

Calls for help won't be dealt with quickly, either. There is a delay of 5 to 20 minutes between Earth and Mars. Spacecraft send radio signals back to Earth. Huge antennas on Earth pick up the signals. If the spacecraft is far away, the signal might be very weak. Engineers find ways to boost the signal and process images and data for scientists.

The Future

Getting people to Mars is exciting to think about. But there are ways to prepare for life on another planet without leaving Earth. There are scientists, astronauts, and researchers right now who are creating and experiencing Mars-like living conditions right here at home.

The cold, snowy, icy continent Antarctica is sometimes called White Mars. It gives us a taste of extreme cold and no rain. Average winter temperatures can fall between –76° and –40° F (–60° and –40° C). Extreme winds of nearly 200 miles (321 km) per hour can whip up dry soil into Mars-like dust storms.

McMurdo is the largest research station in Antarctica. In total, there are 70 permanent stations across the continent.

Getting to Antarctica is challenging, but it is also home to a large scientific research facility, McMurdo Station. Astronauts use the station to practice living in remote areas. They also study the microbes that live on the continent. Microbes have been found in the air, in the water, and deep underneath a frozen lake. The continent is a good model for what life, both human and microbial, would be like on the real Mars.

On the opposite end of the planet, Iceland gives scientists a look at what Mars might have looked like 3.5 billion years ago. Both Mars and Iceland are covered in volcanoes. The volcanoes in Iceland can teach scientists about volcanic activity on Mars. One difference is that Iceland's volcanoes are full of microbes. If microbes can survive near a volcano, maybe they could survive on Mars.

Our Responsibility

Some people have suggested detonating **nuclear bombs** over Mars's poles as a way to get water. The nuclear **radiation** would cause the ice at the poles to melt. Experts believe that there is enough ice at the poles to cover the whole planet with 115 feet (35 m) of water. The melting ice would also release large amounts of water vapor and **carbon dioxide**, which are both **greenhouse gases**. The planet would warm up a lot.

But this idea comes with a lot of questions. Is it okay for us to change a whole planet so we can live there? Does it matter if Mars has life already or not? What if it didn't work or made planet conditions worse? And who will take responsibility if it does make things worse?

[21ST CENTURY SKILLS LIBRARY]

The Pilbara covers 196,100 square miles (507,896 square kilometers) of western Australia.

The Australian Outback is another Mars-like location. The Pilbara region in northwest Australia is home to the oldest fossils on Earth. Scientists study the fossils to find clues about what life on Earth was like 3.5 billion years ago. They will use that information when they hunt for life on Mars. A piece of rock from Pilbara was sent on board with *Perseverance*. The rock helped **calibrate** the rover's tools before it took samples of Mars's rock.

Biodomes are self-contained, self-sustaining environments.

Experts think terraforming Mars could take anywhere from 50 years to 100 million years. That's a huge difference! There are a lot of things to think about. But practicing on Earth is the best way to prepare for life on Mars. Scientists are working on water, oxygen, and other space problems. But ecological habitats and biodomes have been built to give normal people a taste of Martian life. Learning how to live in a small, enclosed space, growing our own food, breathing recycled air, and drinking recycled water are all things we can try out here.

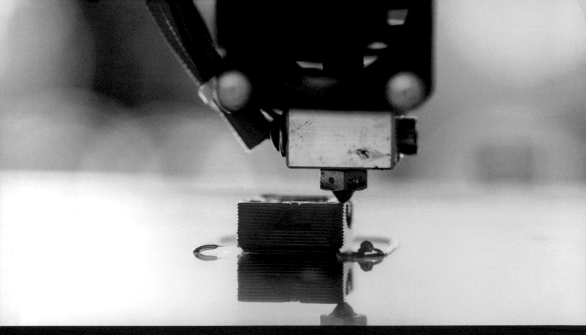

Most 3D printers use plastic. But others use metal, resin, carbon fiber, and other, stronger materials.

Tech Working on Mars

When we think about living on Mars, biodomes are probably what come to mind. But scientists are working on other ways to build places suitable for living. It will be expensive to bring supplies from Earth. It could cost $5,000 per pound to ship things to Mars. One scientist is collecting soil samples in Arizona and turning them into cement. If it works on Earth, the hope is that it would work on Mars, too. Another company has designed 3D-printed houses. A construction rover would use materials on Mars and plastic made from renewable resources to print the parts.

Activity: Make a Map

The HiRISE camera takes pictures of Mars's surface. Then scientists turn those pictures into a terrain map to help rovers watch out for hazardous areas. You can make your own terrain map. Start with a simple area with just a few objects, like a park. Then try somewhere with more items, like your classroom or bedroom.

WHAT YOU'LL NEED:

- **measuring tape**
- **graph paper and pencil**
- **colored pencils**

1. Use the measuring tape to measure your space. Then draw the space on the graph paper. One square equals 1 foot (0.3 m).

2. Use the measuring tape to measure the width of each item in the space. Then draw the items onto your graph paper.

3. Use the measuring tape to measure the height of each item in the space.

4. Color your map in. The lowest points should be blue. The highest points should be red. Middle points should be yellow. Use green and orange to show heights that are in between.

Find Out More

BOOKS

Goldstein, Margaret J. *Elon Musk: Tesla Founder and Titan of Tech.* Minneapolis, MN: Lerner Publications, 2022.

MacCarald, Clara. *Colonizing Mars.* Lake Elmo, MN: Focus Readers, 2020.

Maranville, Amy. *The Apollo 11 Moon Landing: A Day That Changed America.* North Mankato, MN: Capstone Press, 2022.

Owen, Ruth. *Astronauts.* New York, NY: AV2, 2020.

WEBSITES

Curious Kids: Can People Colonize Mars?
https://theconversation.com/curious-kids-can-people-colonize-mars-122251
Read what experts have to say about a future Mars colony.

Mission to Mars
https://kids.nationalgeographic.com/space/article/mission-to-mars
Get some fast facts about the Red Planet.

Mission to Mars!
https://www.mensaforkids.org/teach/lesson-plans/mission-to-mars
Explore the possibility of becoming one of the first people on Mars.

NASA's Mars Exploration Program
https://mars.nasa.gov
Experience up-to-the-minute updates about the Red Planet, from weather to recent discoveries.

GLOSSARY

calibrate (KAL-uh-brayt) to check an instrument's accuracy by testing it against a standard unit of measurement

carbon dioxide (KAR-buhn die-OX-ide) a heavy colorless gas; humans inhale oxygen and exhale carbon dioxide

colonizing (KOL-uh-nyz) sending a group of settlers to a new place

core (KOR) the innermost layers of a planet; cores can be solid, liquid, or both

craters (CRAY-tuhrz) large bowl-shaped depressions in the ground

erosion (uh-ROW-shuhn) worn away gradually by natural means, such as water or ice

flyby (FLY-by) sending a spacecraft within close range of a planet

greenhouse gases (GREEN-hows GASS-uhz) gasses that let sunlight pass through but absorb heat

hazard map (HAZ-ahrd MAP) a map that highlights natural hazards in a particular area, such as rough terrain, flooding, volcanoes, or earthquakes

microbes (MY-krowbs) single-celled microorganisms that are too small to be seen by the naked eye; microbes include bacteria, algae, and amoeba

nuclear bombs (NOO-klee-uhr BOMZ) explosive devices that releases large amounts of energy

orbits (OR-bitz) moves in a circular motion around a planet or other object

orbiter (or-BIT-uhr) a spacecraft designed to orbit a planet

probe (PROHB) an unpiloted spacecraft that travels through space to collect information

radiation (ray-dee-AY-shuhn) a form of energy that travels through space

solar power (SOH-luhr POW-uhr) power gained by harnessing the energy of the Sun's rays

terrain (tuh-RAYN) the physical features of an area

INDEX